Human Rights in Islam

By His Excellency, Sheikh
Saleh bin Abdul Aziz bin Muhammad
bin Ibrahim Aal al-Shaikh

Human Rights in Islam

By His Excellency,
Saleh bin Abdul Aziz bin Muhammad bin Ibrahim Aal al-Shaikh

Translated by

The Translation Centre/KSU

In the Name of Allah, the Most Gracious the Most Merciful

Praise be to Allah the Lord of the universe who says in His perfect Book:

﴿ ۞ وَلَقَدْ كَرَّمْنَا بَنِىٓ ءَادَمَ وَحَمَلْنَٰهُمْ فِى ٱلْبَرِّ وَٱلْبَحْرِ وَرَزَقْنَٰهُم مِّنَ ٱلطَّيِّبَٰتِ وَفَضَّلْنَٰهُمْ عَلَىٰ كَثِيرٍ مِّمَّنْ خَلَقْنَا تَفْضِيلًا ﴿٧٠﴾ ﴾

[الإسراء: ٧٠]

"And indeed We have honoured the Children of Adam, and carried them on land and sea, and provided them with good things, and preferred them above many of those whom We have created with a marked preference."[1]

I praise Allah Almighty, who knows best what He created, and He is well acquainted with all things. I praise the goodness in his commands and prohibitions, His law and His guidance, as He is the one who guided the people and commanded them to

---

[1] *al-Isrā': 70*

do that in which lies their betterment in their worldly life and in the Hereafter. Much praise is due to Him since His bounties upon us are many. I bear witness that there is no deity worthy of worship except Allah alone, without any partner, and I bear witness that Muhammad is His servant and Messenger, may the peace and many blessings of Allah be upon him, his family and companions.

It is a Muslim's duty to take care to learn about the religion what he does not know, and to reaffirm his knowledge about things he might have forgotten with the passage of time, due to the busy pace of life.

There is no doubt that the law of Islam is a perfect and blessed law, and no better legal system has ever come to the people. Allah has given every Prophet a law, and the law he gave to Prophet Muhammad is the most perfect and complete law that will endure until the end of time. It is suitable for all times and places, no matter how diverse.

﴿... ٱلۡيَوۡمَ أَكۡمَلۡتُ لَكُمۡ دِينَكُمۡ وَأَتۡمَمۡتُ عَلَيۡكُمۡ نِعۡمَتِي وَرَضِيتُ لَكُمُ ٱلۡإِسۡلَٰمَ دِينٗاۚ فَمَنِ ٱضۡطُرَّ فِي مَخۡمَصَةٍ غَيۡرَ مُتَجَانِفٖ لِّإِثۡمٖ فَإِنَّ ٱللَّهَ غَفُورٞ رَّحِيمٞ ٣﴾ [المائدة: ٣]

"This day, I have perfected your religion for you, completed My Favour upon you, and have chosen for you Islam as your religion. But as for him who is forced by severe hunger, with no inclination to sin (such can eat these above-mentioned meats), then surely, Allah is Oft-Forgiving, Most Merciful."[1]

Indeed, Islamic law provides a solution for every problem, protection of every right, and the elevation of human dignity on the basis of our common humanity. It honours the Muslims for bearing the message of monotheism. Hence, it becomes incumbent upon everyone to know the merits of this law with its injunctions, objectives and purposes, and the rights it guarantees. This will encourage them to act upon it and call others

---

[1] *al-Mā'idah: 3*

towards it. It will protect them from the distortions and misrepresentations of those who wish to block people from reaching the truth through deceptive means and propaganda.

We praise Allah for making us among those who follow this law, learn it, and emulate the good manners of Allah's Messenger. Having said that, the lectures I delivered in the mosque under the title of "Legal Rights" covered the most important topics that a Muslim should know about. This is because Allah has established the heavens and the Earth upon two sets of rights: His rights and the rights of the people. All the Messengers throughout time and all the revealed scriptures came to explain these two sets of rights: first, Allah's right that we worship Him alone, reject the idolatry, and obey His Messenger whose obedience is required by Him in all times and places; and then that we uphold the rights of the people. This is why Allah revealed the scriptures and sent His Messengers. He says:

﴿ لَقَدْ أَرْسَلْنَا رُسُلَنَا بِٱلْبَيِّنَٰتِ وَأَنزَلْنَا مَعَهُمُ ٱلْكِتَٰبَ وَٱلْمِيزَانَ لِيَقُومَ ٱلنَّاسُ بِٱلْقِسْطِ ... ﴾ [الحديد: ٢٥]

"Indeed, We have sent Our Messengers with clear proofs, and revealed with them the Scripture and the Balance so that humankind may uphold justice."[1]

He also says:

﴿ وَلَقَدْ بَعَثْنَا فِى كُلِّ أُمَّةٍ رَّسُولًا أَنِ ٱعْبُدُوا۟ ٱللَّهَ وَٱجْتَنِبُوا۟ ٱلطَّٰغُوتَ ... ﴾ [النحل: ٣٦]

"And verily, We have sent among every nation a Messenger (proclaiming): 'Worship Allah (alone), and avoid all false deities."[2]

For the same reason, the Prophet said to Mu'adh, "O Mu'adh, do you know what Allah's right is upon His servants and what the servants' rights are upon Allah?"

---

[1] *al-Hadīd: 25*

[2] *al-Nahl: 36*

Mu'adh said: "Allah and His Messenger know the best."

The Prophet said: "Indeed Allah's right upon His servants is that they should worship Him and not associate any partner with Him. The servants' right upon Allah is that He should not punish those who do not associate any partner with Him."

Mu'adh said: "O Messenger of Allah, shouldn't I go and give this good news to the people?"

He said: "Do not give this good news to them, because they might depend upon it to the exclusion of all else."[1]

Hence, the rights brought by all the divinely revealed laws, and by Islamic law in particular, are the right of Allah and the rights of the people. This will be manifest for you when you will reflect upon the Book of Allah regarding this topic as well as the Prophet's life and Sunnah.

---

1 Narrated by Bukhari (2856) and Muslim (30).

Regarding the rights enshrined in Islamic law, scholars of Islam have propounded upon them at length. Among the rights discussed frequently in our present day are what are called 'Human Rights'. This topic, which I have made the title of this book, has been the focus of considerable academic research form a variety of angles, including the standpoint of Islamic law, Islamic beliefs, how they relate to the Muslim judiciary, as well as their political and economic dimensions in Islam.

This topic is a serious concern for all the major countries of the world, as seen in the United Nations' 'Human Rights Conventions'. The creation of the term 'Human Rights' has a story behind it. It is a relatively new term. It is not found in Islamic law, nor in the Qur'an and Sunnah, nor in earlier scholarly discourse. However, its meaning is very much present in the Qur'an and Sunnah, which can be seen by reviewing the rights addressed under Islamic law.

After the American-led allied victory in the Second World War, the United Nations established the new world order. The term "new world order" is not the product of the aftermath of Gulf war; but rather has its origins after the Second World War. It was devised so that the great and powerful countries could use it whenever they wanted to impose something new upon other nations and peoples regardless of their various cultures and national boundaries. After the Second World War, they wanted a new world order through which the powerful countries could control all other countries. This control sometimes took the form of cultural interventions, sometimes it related to the assurance of freedoms, sometimes it took the form of direct intervention in other countries' affairs. A part of this new world order was the United Nations' Universal Declaration of Human Rights in 1948, which has 30 articles, later followed by a number of amendments and additions. This document – with all its additions – is now called the International Bill of Human Rights.

Human rights, as conceptualised by the United Nations and the countries of the western world, refer back to two essential concepts:freedom and equality.

Freedom means, inter alia, the abolition of slavery in all its guises, considering it an illegitimate act. It also means the development of a detailed discourse on freedom, categorising its various manifestations, like individual freedom, political freedom, financial freedom, freedom of the judiciary, and the right to national identity.

Equality was addressed in equal detail, including matters such as gender, race, ethnicity and social class. It also addressed questions of people's rights and choices, and their choosing the country wherein they wish to live.

Therefore, all human rights, as conceptualised by the United Nations, are related to two important principles: freedom and equality.

Among the articles of the Universal Declaration of Human Rights are those that prohibit certain activities and limit the right of state in how it relates to the people. In this way, western countries and the United Nations interfered in the internal affairs of many countries and imposed many things on them. Statements were often made against countries for not upholding certain rights.Sometimes the interference becomes greater and countries were called into question on their human rights record and made to account for what they have done to ensure these freedoms, citing individual cases. They also broached political freedoms, while calling towards democracy and the rule of the people. This is why elections and parliaments throughout the world are established on western models.

There is no doubt that when these principles are imposed from outside upon nations whose people lack a sufficient understanding of them, those nations will be easy to manipulate and control, and can be placed under the power of those who are friendly to the West. This is especially true of the liberation and independence movements that rejected colonial rule in the wake of the Second World War. The general call for human rights took place in a specific historical context that served the interests of the major colonial powers.

When the topic of human rights is discussed, Muslims should feel proud of their religion and be certain that a human right is greater when it is from Allah who best knows His creatures and what is good for them. Allah says:

﴿ أَلَا يَعْلَمُ مَنْ خَلَقَ وَهُوَ ٱللَّطِيفُ ٱلْخَبِيرُ ﴿١٤﴾ ﴾ [الملك: ١٤]

"Should not He Who has created know? And He is the Most Kind and Courteous (to His slaves) All-Aware (of everything)."[1]

Allah is the one who protects human rights through His law. He protects the rights of the people regardless of how different they are. Many people who have written on the issue of 'Human Rights' have demonstrated that Islamic law, the biography of

[1] *al-Mulk: 14*

our Prophet Muhammad, the injunctions in the Qur'an and Sunnah, the deeds of the four rightly guided Caliphs and those who came after them, constitute the greatest early document of 'Human Rights' which is well-developed in both theory and practice. This is because as the principles of human rights were fully implemented during the time of the Prophet and during the time of the four rightly guided Caliphs. Thus, many researchers wrote about this topic and among topic them, there are some who viewed the UN Declaration of Human Rights uncritically, and tried to find for each and every section of that declaration a precedence in the Islamic history or Islamic law. They focused particularly on the abolishment of slavery and equality of men and women. The weakness in their approach is still seen in many researchers who are facing western allegations or trying to find an Islamic precedence for a particular interpretation of certain rights or freedoms.

Other researchers approached the issue objectively, usually writing academic articles and publishing in journals, where they explained that some of the human rights as understood in the West and articulated by the United Nations, are affirmed by Islamic law in exactly the same way while others are incongruous with Islamic teachings to a greater or lesser extent. Allah has commanded Muslims to refer all matters of disagreement back to Him, where He says:

﴿ وَأَنِ ٱحْكُم بَيْنَهُم بِمَآ أَنزَلَ ٱللَّهُ وَلَا تَتَّبِعْ أَهْوَآءَهُمْ وَٱحْذَرْهُمْ أَن يَفْتِنُوكَ عَنۢ بَعْضِ مَآ أَنزَلَ ٱللَّهُ إِلَيْكَ ۖ ... ﴾ [المائدة: ٤٩]

"And so judge (you O Muhammad) between them by what Allah has revealed and follow not their vain desires, but beware of them lest they turn you (O Muhammad) far away from some of that which Allah has sent down to you."[1]

[1] *al-Mā'idah: 49*

He also says:

﴿... إِنِ ٱلْحُكْمُ إِلَّا لِلَّهِ أَمَرَ أَلَّا تَعْبُدُوٓا۟ إِلَّآ إِيَّاهُ ...﴾

[يوسف: ٤٠]

"The command (or the judgement) is for none but Allah. He has commanded that you worship none but Him (i.e. His Monotheism)."[1]

This command to refer to Allah in matters of disagreement applies to questions of academic importance as well as to practical matters.

The present book might not cover all aspects of the topic of human rights, but we will try to clarify the topic enough so that the reader will understand the Islamic legal principles of 'Human Rights' and compare them to those of the West. This should lead to an appreciation of how human rights are contextualised according to the wishes of colonizers and those who are hostile towards Islam, and that adopting such a contextualisation of human

---

[1] *Yūsuf: 40*

rights is not in the best interest of Islam and the Muslims. Quite the contrary, it can lead to interference in their affairs and cause them to deviate from their religious values, and consequently lead them to blindly follow the West in its understanding of freedoms,equality,the proper relationship between men and women, financial affairs, and political agendas.

The Origin of Human Rights

The topic of human rights in Islam can be referred back to Allah's statement:

﴿ ۞ وَلَقَدْ كَرَّمْنَا بَنِيٓ ءَادَمَ ... ﴾ [الإسراء: ٧٠]

"And indeed We have honoured the Children of Adam."[1]

Allah's respect for the children of Adam, as the scholars have stated, refers to two things:

First: Allah's respect for the children of Adam in their structure, physical creation, and in whatever

---

[1] *al-Isrā': 70*

He provided for them in the heaven and on Earth. This is addressed directly in the verse.

Second: Allah has elevated the children of Adam above the animals and other creations and preferred them above many of His creatures in all that is related to their happiness and interests, through what they seek in their livelihood and in their relationships with their fellow human beings. For this very reason, different laws were revealed to explain to them the rights of Allah and the rights of the people. Therefore, after Allah declares:

﴿ ۞ وَلَقَدْ كَرَّمْنَا بَنِيٓ ءَادَمَ ... ﴾ [الإسراء: ٧٠]

"And indeed We have honoured the Children of Adam."

He continues, saying:

﴿ ... وَفَضَّلْنَٰهُمْ عَلَىٰ كَثِيرٍ مِّمَّنْ خَلَقْنَا تَفْضِيلًا ﴿٧٠﴾ ﴾

[الإسراء: ٧٠]

"...and have preferred them above many of

those whom We have created with a marked preference."[1]

This refers not only to the creation of humanity, but also to the promulgation of the human race and the organization of human society. It also refers to the fact that they have been called upon to worship Allah alone and to follow the prophets and messengers.

We have already discussed that in the West, and among those influenced by the West, the rights that come under the term 'Human Rights' are of two kinds: freedom and equality. The freedom that they call towards does not exist in an unqualified sense, even in their own countries. This is because unqualified freedom means that people can do whatever they want and this does not exist anywhere in the world. Throughout the world, freedoms have their limits. When the limit is reached, it is said that you need to stop here; you are not free to go beyond this. This should give you the understanding that the

---

[1] *al-Isrā': 70*

term freedom exists only in a relative sense. Absolute freedom in everything; in money, politics, the judiciary, human life, and family, does not exist anywhere in the world. The freedom that is available in the world varies in its degree from country to country based on the strength with which freedoms are granted.

Therefore, the word 'freedom' that constitutes part of the "Human Rights" they call towards, is not available with them without limits. If this is the case, *i.e.* if they put human limits on it based on their opinions, then we may say that this principal shows that putting a limit on freedom has negated the idea that the word 'freedom' is equally acceptable to every human being. If freedom has to be accepted and relied upon, then human beings should be granted their freedom in whatever they want. In this way you will be calling towards unlimited freedom. But if you limit it by granting a certain kind of freedom and limit openly through legislation and subtly through covert checks on people's wealth and capabilities then it is not accepted that there is unlimited freedom.

So the basis for the freedom that is called to in their conceptualisation of "Human Rights" must be looked at from the angle that the freedom is not without limits; rather it is necessarily limited, meaning that human beings are not totally free anywhere on the Earth to do as they please. Instead, they have limits prescribed for them and described to them in detail. This is why protocols and etiquettes were introduced, and other measures were introduced to stop people who do not abide by them from participating in official business or entering any place in casual clothes or attending any place or saying anything.

There is a lack of freedom prevailing everywhere. This is because it is deemed that it is not appropriate that people should be given their freedom due to its contradicting good taste sometime or due to its impairing social relationships, or due to it contravening the rights of others. Hence the idea of giving full freedom in the "Human Rights" is negated in principle.

Secondly, the equality they are calling towards means equality between men and women in everything. It also means equality of all people in the taking and giving of rights, in wages, in education, health, medical care, travelling and living wherever they wish in their country – as their articles say – , the abolition of slavery… etc.

In this conceptualisation of equality, there are some things which are acceptable and others which are not, which we will be discussing, God willing. Our purpose here is not to criticize the declaration and its amendments. Rather, we are here to make clear that the most complete and noble manifestation of human rights is that which is granted by the Lord of humanity.

When people wish to give rights to someone, they will never be safe from the influence of their desires . Regardless of who the legislators are, their desires will interfere. This is why we see that western laws, like those of France or America, are subject to change with the passage of time, either due to some particular interests present at the time the laws were first enacted, or due to the power of influential people,or due to changes in circumstances over time. In this regard, Allah has told that decisions made in the time of ignorance are based on people's vain desires. Allah says:

﴿ وَأَنِ ٱحْكُم بَيْنَهُم بِمَآ أَنزَلَ ٱللَّهُ وَلَا تَتَّبِعْ أَهْوَآءَهُمْ ... ﴾

[المائدة: ٤٩]

"And so judge (you O Muhammad) between them by what Allah has revealed and follow not their vain desires."[1]

Hence, every decision that is not in conformity with Islamic law is no doubt based on vain desires and not in conformity with what is correct.

People's desires certainly prevent them from giving others their rights properly. Therefore, the

[1] *al-Mā'idah: 49*

principles they devised are based on a human vision which was influenced by desires and dictated by the interests of the countries involved and their desire to control weaker countries or countries possessing resources.

If you consider the state of the people before the advent of Prophet Muhammad, whether they were Arabs – the Arabs of Mecca and its surroundings – or those who were elsewhere in the Arabian Peninsula or those who were in Syria, Egypt, Iran and Rome, you will find that depriving people of their freedoms was commonplace. There was no equality whatsoever. The law of jungle prevailed. The strong devoured the weak and people oppressed one another.

When Rib'ee went to the chief of Persian army, the chief asked him: "What brought you here?"

He replied: "Allah has sent us out to release whomever He wills from the worship of people to the worship of Allah and from the constriction of this world to its vastness and from the injustice of the religious systems to the justice of Islam".[1]

When the Prophet came, Allah revealed the law of Islam to him and ordered him to proclaim the truth and warn his close relatives then warn all of humanity. Allah made his messengership a mercy for the whole world. He says:

﴿ وَمَآ أَرۡسَلۡنَٰكَ إِلَّا رَحۡمَةٗ لِّلۡعَٰلَمِينَ ١٠٧ ﴾

[الأنبياء: ١٠٧]

"And We have sent you (O Muhammad) not but as a mercy for all the worlds."[2]

When the Prophet came to that society, it was a society where class conflict was rife and the class discrimination was at its worst. It was a society where this tribe was better than that one, these individuals were more illustrious than those, and some were entitled to control the affairs of others.

1- See: Tarikh al-Tabari, Vol. 3, page 520, and al-Bidayah wa al-Nihayah, Vol. 7, page 46.

[2] *al-Anbiyā': 107*

These were the tribal traditions where discrimination and favouritism among people was the order of the day.

The Prophet brought a great principal to them, expressed in the Qur'an where Allah says:

﴿ يَٰٓأَيُّهَا ٱلنَّاسُ إِنَّا خَلَقۡنَٰكُم مِّن ذَكَرٖ وَأُنثَىٰ وَجَعَلۡنَٰكُمۡ شُعُوبٗا وَقَبَآئِلَ لِتَعَارَفُوٓاْۚ إِنَّ أَكۡرَمَكُمۡ عِندَ ٱللَّهِ أَتۡقَىٰكُمۡ ... ﴾ [الحجرات: ١٣]

"O humankind! We have created you from a male and a female, and made you into nations and tribes, that you may know one another. Verily, the most honourable of you with Allah are those who are most God-fearing."[1]

Piety became the only criterion for true nobility, preference and excellence.These traits were not based on gender, colour, tribe or nationality, but inner goodness:

﴿ ... إِنَّ أَكۡرَمَكُمۡ عِندَ ٱللَّهِ أَتۡقَىٰكُمۡ ... ﴾

---

[1] *al-Hujurāt: 13*

“Verily, the most honourable of you with Allah are those who are most God-fearing."

Likewise, our Prophet said: 'O people! Behold, your Lord is one, and your father is one. Behold, no Arab is superior to a non-Arab, nor is a non-Arab is superior to an Arab, nor is a white person superior to a black person, nor is a black person superior to a white person except with piety."[1]

It is also narrated in a tradition that he said: 'People are as equal as the teeth of a comb. They are preferred over each other by their goodness.'[2] This is referring to the responsibilities where Allah has made people equal by addressing them with the commandments of Islam. In this, there is no difference between male and female, free and slave, or rich and poor.All people are commanded to believe in the oneness of Allah and to obey Him and fear Him according to their ability.This is a complete

---

1 It is narrated by Ahmad (38/474), and al-Baihaqi in Shu'ab al-Iman (7/132), and Abu Nu'aim in al-Hilyah (3/100).

2 It is narrated by al-Quda'ee in his Musnad (1/145), and al-Asbahani in his book al-Amthal fi al-Hadith al-Nabawi (p. 203).

equality in this responsibility.

Similarly, when Islam came, it put an end to discrimination among people, making them brothers to each other. The Prophet made every immigrant form Mecca a brother to a person from the city of Madina where the Meccan Muslims went to seeking refuge. He also established this brotherhood between free people and slaves in Madina. It is narrated by Ali that the Prophet considered Salman the Persian one of his family members. It is an authentic narration from Ali that the Prophet peace be on him said: 'Salman is from us, he is a member of the family.'[1] This tradition is narrated as a statement of the Prophet, but it is authentic as a statement of Ali.

This equality and lack of discrimination between the people is among the noblest things that

---

1 It is narrated by Tabarani in al-Kabir (6/212), and Hakem (3/691), and ibn Abi Shaiba in his Musannaf (12/148), and ibn Sa'd (2/346, 4/85), and Abu Nu'aim in al-Hilyah (1/87), and ibn 'Asakir (7/411, 415). Albani authenticated this tradition as Mawqoof and considered it as unauthentic as Marfoo'. See: al-Silsilah al-Dha'eefah (3704).

Islam pioneered in the field of human rights, as it gave people their rights on the basis of being the children of Adam. All humanity is equal in their rights before Allah and they are also equal in giving others their rights and fulfilling their duties between themselves and among the people.

The Prophet made Zaid bin Haritha, a freed slave, the leader of a large military force and then made Zaid's son Usama the leader after him. Abu Bakr al-Siddiq maintained that appointment during his reign.

When the Muslims spread Islam into the surrounding countries, non-Arabs – Persians and others – became scholars of Islam and imams of the mosques, and they started teaching the people and sharing their knowledge. It is recorded in Islamic history that many non-Arabs led the Muslims in knowledge and in issuing legal verdicts and many other things. Take, for example, their leadership in knowledge. Abu Hanifa was not an Arab, nor was Imam Bukhari, whose hadith compilation is the most important work in the field. There is not a single Muslim who does not know Imam Abu Abdullah Muhammad bin Isma'il al-Bukhari and there is a long list of non-Arabs who are among the leading scholars of Islam. So when Islam came, it abolished all kinds of discrimination and these non-Arabs became leaders and imams ahead of the Arabs. How could they do so? It is because they studied the religion and carried the banner of monotheism: "There is no deity except Allah and Muhammad is the Messenger of Allah". There is no difference between a non-Arab and an Arab except due to piety.

When the Muslims learned Islamic etiquettes, they did not have the problem of class discrimination. They did not prefer the religious leadership of one class or nationality over another. Rather, they accepted everyone, as the people are equal in this respect.

When the rein of Ummayyads and Abbasids ended, which were dynasties from the Arab tribe of Quraysh, the Mamluk dynasty came to power, and they had been former slaves. Then the Turkish Ottoman rulers came to power, and they were good rulers during the early years of their rule. The Muslims followed them, because those leaders and governors considered the lawful interests of the people and the people's welfare was realised.

Hence, Islam was the first system to abolish class discrimination and make it a practical reality for the people. Islamic history is full examples where this great principal, the principal of equality, was put into practice. History is a witness on it.

Regarding the principle of equality in rights, there is no doubt that Islamic law has realised it in a most comprehensive manner. There are two important values in Islamic Law that need to be discussed:

1: Equality

2: Justice

Justice is mandatory under all circumstances, while equality is practiced where it is appropriate.

Equality is not absolute. In other words, justice means to give everyone their due and extend to them all of their rights without any abuse or transgression. This is justice, and Allah has commanded us categorically to do justice. He says:

﴿إِنَّ ٱللَّهَ يَأۡمُرُ بِٱلۡعَدۡلِ وَٱلۡإِحۡسَٰنِ وَإِيتَآيِٕ ذِي ٱلۡقُرۡبَىٰ ...﴾

[النحل: ٩٠]

"Verily,Allah enjoins justice and good dealings and giving help to kith and kin."[1]

Justice necessitates that all people are given their due rights. No one should be deprived of their rights because of who they are. People should be given the rights they are entitled to on account of their circumstances. This is the reason why Islamic law does not apply strict equality in punishments for crimes that do not have fixed punishments prescribed for them in the Qur'an. The Prophet said: "Forgive honourable people their mistakes except

[1] *al-Nahl: 90*

for crimes with prescribed punishments."[1] Here, there is lack of equality in consideration of the greater societal welfare that is realised by this policy. Umar did not give entitlements equally to others what he gave to the veterans of the Battle of Badr. He also did not give equally from the national welfare funds to those who were first and foremost in accepting Islam and those who accepted Islam later on. Rather, he gave each and everyone their due right according to the sacrifices they had made. This is justice, since treating people equally who differed in their level of sacrifice and commitment in helping Islam would be unjust.

Equality is commanded by Islamic law in numerous rights, like the right to equal treatment before the law in the courtroom and before the state. People should be equal before their governors and

---

1 It is narrated by Abu Dawood (4375), Ahmad (42/300), An-Nasa'ee in al-Kubraa (7253), At-Tahawi in Sharh Mushkil al-Athaar (2377), Abu Nu'aim in al-Hilya (9/43), Baihaqi in Al-Sunan al-Kubraa (8/579, 580), Tabarani in al-Awsat (3/277) and ibn Adi in al-Kamil 5/1945).

judges. The judge should not prefer one person over another. Even if a Muslim and a non-Muslim come before the court, the judge should not discriminate between them, because this is the place of justice and judgment where all people are equal. It is an absolute right that their legal rights should be protected by the force of the judiciary. Allah says:

﴿... فَإِن جَآءُوكَ فَٱحۡكُم بَيۡنَهُمۡ أَوۡ أَعۡرِضۡ عَنۡهُمۡۖ وَإِن تُعۡرِضۡ عَنۡهُمۡ فَلَن يَضُرُّوكَ شَيۡـٔٗاۖ ...﴾ [المائدة: ٤٢]

"So if they come to you (O Muhammad), either judge between them, or turn away from them. If you turn away from them, they cannot hurt you in the least."[1]

This refers to the Jews and Christians.

﴿... وَإِنۡ حَكَمۡتَ فَٱحۡكُم بَيۡنَهُم بِٱلۡقِسۡطِۚ إِنَّ ٱللَّهَ يُحِبُّ ٱلۡمُقۡسِطِينَ ٤٢﴾ [المائدة: ٤٢]

---

[1] *al-Mā'idah: 42*

"And if you judge, judge with justice between them. Verily, Allah loves those who act justly."[1]

The idea that everyone is equal in having their rights rendered to them was proclaimed by Prophet Muhammad in the clearest possible manner on many occasions. For instance, he mentioned how the Jews came to ruin because they discriminated between their nobles and commoners in laws, judicial procedures, and punishing criminal offences. The Prophet said: "I swear by Allah, that even if Fatima the daughter of Muhammad stole, I would have cut off her hand."[2] Hence the lives, wealth and honour of all people are valued and protected equally. So there is no difference between anyone in the sanctity of their lives and reputations. Likewise, all people's property rights are equally protected in Islamic law and in the courts. Perhaps this is why the Prophet allowed someone to hit him back when he hurt him by mistake in the battle of Badr. Usaid bin Hudhair

---

[1] *al-Mā'idah: 42*

2 It is narrated by Bukhari (3475) and Muslim (1688).

narrates that while the Prophet was talking to the people and making them laugh, he hit him lightly on his waist with a stick. When he complained, the Prophet said: “You may take your revenge.” He said: “I will.” Then he said: “You are wearing a shirt but there is not shirt on my body.” The Prophet then lifted his shirt for him. He came forward, hugged him, kissed his flank and said: “I intended only this, O Messenger of Allah."[1]

The Prophet said on another occasion while praying for his community:"O Allah!If I insulted any believer, then make it a good deed for him on the Day of Judgment."[2]

Therefore, people are equal in their judicial rights regardless of whether they are Muslims or non-Muslims. Their right before the courts and their rights in Islamic law are the same.We do not take the right of a Christian and give it to a Muslim or of a Jew and give it to a Muslim. Rights are only

---

1 It is narrated by Abu Dawood (5224), Tabarani in al-Kabir (1/205,206), Hakim (3/327) and al-Baihaqi in al-Kubra (8/78).

2 It is narrated by Bukhari (6361) and Muslim (2600).

transferred by the courts on the basis of legal evidence. "Give the trust to the one who has entrusted you and do not be untrustworthy to the one who was untrustworthy to you."[1] Allah says:

﴿ وَأَنِ ٱحْكُم بَيْنَهُم بِمَآ أَنزَلَ ٱللَّهُ ... ﴾ [المائدة: ٤٩]

"And so judge (you O Muhammad) between them by what Allah has revealed."[2]

Allah has commanded us to be firm in justice, witnesses for Allah, even if it is against our own selves:

﴿ ۞ يَـٰٓأَيُّهَا ٱلَّذِينَ ءَامَنُوا۟ كُونُوا۟ قَوَّٰمِينَ بِٱلْقِسْطِ شُهَدَآءَ لِلَّهِ وَلَوْ عَلَىٰٓ أَنفُسِكُمْ ... ﴾ [النساء: ١٣٥]

"O you who believe! Stand out firmly for justice, as witnesses to Allah, even though it be

---

1 It is narrated by Abu Dawood (3534), Tirmidhi (1264), Darimi (2693), Ahmad (24/150), al-Baihaqi in his Sunan (10/456), Dar Qutni (3/443), Hakim (2/53), Tahawi in Sharh Mushkil al-Athaar (5/91,95), Tabarani in al-Kabir (1/288, 8/127) and in al-Awsat (4/55) and in al-Saghir (475), and Abu Nu'aim in al-Hilyah (6/132).

2 al-Mā'idah: 49

against yourselves."[1]

He also says:

﴿... وَلَا يَجْرِمَنَّكُمْ شَنَـَٔانُ قَوْمٍ عَلَىٰٓ أَلَّا تَعْدِلُوا۟ ٱعْدِلُوا۟ هُوَ أَقْرَبُ لِلتَّقْوَىٰ ...﴾ [المائدة: ٨]

"And let not the enmity and hatred of others make you swerve from justice. Be just: that is nearer to piety."[2]

A Jew would come with a Muslim to the court of law in the era of the Prophet's Companions, and the Muslim would not be given any preference over the Jew in court. Rather, both were just considered as litigants, hence equal. Otherwise, it would lead to injustice. Why? Because if discrimination is found in these case, it will surely lead to corruption on Earth, while Allah has ordered us to reform the world and prohibited us to corrupt it. Allah says:

---

[1] *al-Nisā': 135*

[2] *al-Mā'idah: 8*

﴿ وَلَا تُفْسِدُوا فِي الْأَرْضِ بَعْدَ إِصْلَاحِهَا وَادْعُوهُ خَوْفًا وَطَمَعًا ... ﴾ [الأعراف: ٥٦]

"And do not do mischief on the Earth, after it has been set in order, and invoke Him with fear and hope."[1]

The reformation of the world is achieved through knowledge, through the message of Muhammad, and by giving people their legal rights that our Prophet came with. This is how reform and betterment can come to the world. The greatest aspect of this is monotheism and avoiding false worship. Corruption on Earth happens first when the right of Allah is neglected and then when the rights of the people are abused.[2] This corruption creeps upon society slowly and ultimately invites the wrath of Allah, as He says:

---

[1] *al-A`rāf: 56*

2- See: Ibn Abi Hatim in his Tafseer (1/1501, 5/1520). Imam al-Suyuti, in his book al-Durr al-Manthoor (3/476, 477), attributed this narration to Abu al-Shaikh in Tafseer.

﴿ كُلُوا۟ مِن طَيِّبَٰتِ مَا رَزَقْنَٰكُمْ وَلَا تَطْغَوْا۟ فِيهِ فَيَحِلَّ عَلَيْكُمْ غَضَبِى ۖ وَمَن يَحْلِلْ عَلَيْهِ غَضَبِى فَقَدْ هَوَىٰ ﴿٨١﴾ وَإِنِّى لَغَفَّارٌ لِّمَن تَابَ وَءَامَنَ وَعَمِلَ صَٰلِحًا ثُمَّ ٱهْتَدَىٰ ﴿٨٢﴾ ﴾ [طه: ٨١ – ٨٢]

"Eat of the good things We have provided for you, and commit no oppression therein, lest My anger should justly descend on you. And those on whom My anger descends are indeed fallen. But truly, I am forgiving to those who repent, believe, and do righteous good deeds, and then remain constant in guidance."[1]

In Islam, people, whether in Muslim countries or elsewhere in the world, are characterised as follows:

1: Muslims

2. Non-Muslims living as citizens of the Muslim state, *e.g.* the Jews and Christians who are under the protection of a Muslim state. Their

[1] *Tāhā: 81-82*

circumstances are defined in detail by the jurists.

3. Those who have entered into a covenant with a Muslim state.

4. Those who are at peace with the Muslims.

5. Those who are at war with the Muslims.

So if you want to count the kinds of the non-Muslims living on Earth, then there are four categories; those living as citizens of the Muslim state, those who entered a covenant, those who are at peace with the Muslims, and those who are at war with them. The Prophet ordered that all of these people are to be given their rights. Indeed, Allah has commanded in His Book that the rights of the non-Muslims are to be given to them, provided they are not openly engaging in hostility against the Muslims. He says:

﴿ لَا يَنْهَىٰكُمُ ٱللَّهُ عَنِ ٱلَّذِينَ لَمْ يُقَٰتِلُوكُمْ فِى ٱلدِّينِ وَلَمْ يُخْرِجُوكُم مِّن دِيَٰرِكُمْ
أَن تَبَرُّوهُمْ وَتُقْسِطُوٓا۟ إِلَيْهِمْ ۚ إِنَّ ٱللَّهَ يُحِبُّ ٱلْمُقْسِطِينَ ﴿٨﴾ إِنَّمَا يَنْهَىٰكُمُ ٱللَّهُ عَنِ
ٱلَّذِينَ قَٰتَلُوكُمْ فِى ٱلدِّينِ وَأَخْرَجُوكُم مِّن دِيَٰرِكُمْ وَظَٰهَرُوا۟ عَلَىٰٓ إِخْرَاجِكُمْ أَن تَوَلَّوْهُمْ ۚ
وَمَن يَتَوَلَّهُمْ فَأُو۟لَٰٓئِكَ هُمُ ٱلظَّٰلِمُونَ ﴿٩﴾ ﴾ [الممتحنة: ٨ – ٩]

"Allah does not forbid you to deal justly and kindly with those who did not fight against you on account of your religion nor drive you out of your homes. Verily, Allah loves those who deal with equity. It is only with regards to those who fought against you on account of your religion, and drove you out of your homes, and helped to drive you out, that Allah forbids you to turn to them in allegiance them. And whosoever allies with them, they are the wrongdoers."[1]

---

[1] *al-Mumtahanah: 8-9*

The right of non-Muslim citizens are confirmed in Islamic law. People's disbelief in Islam does not allow us misappropriate their human rights. Their rights are given to them by Allah. The Prophet said: "Whoever kills a non-Muslim citizen will not smell the fragrance of Paradise, though its fragrance extends for a distance of a journey of forty years."[1]

He also said: "Whoever kills a person with whom we have a covenant will not smell the fragrance of Paradise, though its fragrance extends for a distance of a journey of forty years."[2]

Why? Because the covenants of the Muslims must be respected by all Muslims. These people have come with a covenant, a peace treaty, to the Muslim state. They can live in peace and their lives, honour and property are protected. Their rights are firmly protected to them by law. There are many textual evidences that confirm to the rights of non-

---

1 Narrated by Ahmad (11/256), inb Majah (2686), Nasa'ee in al-Mujtaba (8/25) and in al-Kubra (8742), al-Hakim (2/126), al-Baihaqi in al-Sunan (9/205) and ibn Abi Shaibah (9/426).

2 Narrated by Bukahri (3166).

Muslim citizens, those with a covenant and those under protection. The scholars have spoken in detail regarding these issues.

Regarding those who are at war with the Muslims, there are many rulings concerning them. If they are taken as prisoners of war, they are given respect. If they are overpowered, their women, children, and elderly people are not killed.[1] These are among many examples of Islam's humanitarian rulings concerning war. Some other legal systems command that all the captives be killed. For instance, it is mentioned in the Law of Moses that all

1 As it is narrated in a Hadith quoted by Imam Muslim (1731) on the authority of Buraida, may Allah be pleased with him, who said: Whenever the Messenger of Allah appointed a leader over an army or a detachment, he advised him privately to fear Allah and be nice to the Muslim under him, then he said: fight in the name of Allah, in the cause of Allah, fight those who disbelieve in Allah, fight but do not steel from the war booty, do not betray, do not damage the dead bodies, and do not kill a child". Hadith of Atyyah al-Qurazi who said: I was one of the captives from bani Quraiza. They looked, so whoever had grown pubic hair was killed and who did not have was not killed. I was among those who did not have the pubic hair grown. Narrated by Abu Dawood (4404), Tirmidhi (1584), ibn Majah (2541) and Nasa'ee (3430, 4981).

enemies are killed in the state of war. However, Islamic law, which Allah has chosen to remain until the Day of Judgment, says that enemy combatants can only be killed on the battlefield. If they are captured,then there are many other rulings governing their treatment.

Regarding the Muslim citizens of an Islamic State, they have many rights. If they are at home, they may do anything they wish, as long as they do not make public any activities that are considered unlawful among the Muslims. Those who come into the Muslim lands under a covenant are not allowed to propagate their religion. As for the non-Muslim citizens, there are detailed rulings. For instance in lands that have come under Muslim rule, like Syria, Iraq, and Egypt, there are many churches. By contrast, in areas like Saudi Arabia, they are not allowed to make public their religious tenets, like ringing church bells and wearing visible crosses. Likewise, they are not allowed to publicly drink wine. If they wish to drink wine, they may do so privately within their homes. Islamic law protects this right for them, but they are not allowed to make public in Muslim countries things that are against Islamic law. If they do so privately, they will not be investigated for that.

Regarding their financial practices, it is narrated that the non-Muslim traders used to come to Madina for trade and request Umar to allow them to stay there. He used to allow them there and in other cities but never allowed them to stay for more than three nights in the Arabian Peninsula due to the Prophet's prohibition of allowing non-Muslims to reside permanently in the Arabian Peninsula. Non-Muslims have full financial rights to trade and get financial benefits and other financial rights.

Hence, it becomes manifest to you from this brief presentation that Islamic law grants financial rights, equality and justice in many areas. The best examples of giving these rights can be found during the time of the Prophet, and then during the era of his rightly guided Caliphs. This is one kind.

Regarding the second value related to human rights, which is freedom, as we have mentioned, it is always qualified. There are various kinds of personal freedom that we can identify for study, including financial freedom, freedom of travel, and freedom to reside where one wishes. There is political freedom, where people can express their political views and religious freedom which means that people may choose any religion they wish to believe in. These freedoms are addressed by human rights conventions.

In Islamic law, freedom is not absolute, because granting people absolute freedom will lead them to act in any way they wish, which would be contrary to the public interest. It is very well known that the public interest, or the interest of society, is given priority over individual interests. This is a point upon which all legal systems agree. Islam and Islamic law have guaranteed a great degree of freedom for people in many cases, but in a way that it benefits the well-being of the people, which Islam came to ensure. It is well known that Islamic law has come to ensure human welfare and prevent or reduce what is harmful. Islamic law seeks to protect the five necessities of life which are essential for human life to thrive. These are: religion, life, property, reason, and dignity. These are the five necessities that Islam came to protect. With these considerations in mind, Islamic law gives people a great degree of freedom to act as they wish.

Among the forms of freedom that Islam guarantees for all people freedom in their financial undertakings, provided they are sane and have the mental capacity to act in their own interests. If they wish to spoil their wealth and harm themselves, then they will be stopped from doing so. These considerations come under the topic of "legal competence". For instance, if an old man misuses his wealth, instead of saving it for himself and his children and instead of making good use of it so he runs the risk of destitution, his children or relatives can object to his actions, and he can be prevented from using his money in this way.

Similarly a young orphan, if he inherits a great amount of wealth, is not given the opportunity to waste him money. An eight or ten year old child cannot buy a car according to his wishes or travel as he wishes using his money. Islamic law requires that a guardian is appointed to manage the orphan's money in a way that is the best for the orphan. Allah says:

﴿...فَإِنْ ءَانَسْتُم مِّنْهُمْ رُشْدًا فَادْفَعُوٓا۟ إِلَيْهِمْ أَمْوَٰلَهُمْ ...﴾

[النساء: ٦]

"If then you find sound judgement in them, release their property to them."[1]

Sound judgement means knowing how to properly use wealth. It is a great financial freedom that people may own any lawful thing. When it comes to spending according to their free will, they may purchase things, give gifts, lend money, and

[1] *al-Nisā': 6*

travel as long as they have the mental competence to act in their own interests and in the interests of their dependents. If they are not able to do so, then their freedom will be reduced. The reason this freedom is curtailed here is due to the harm that those of limited mental competence will otherwise cause themselves. If a person wants to harm himself, it becomes obligatory upon all to take care of his interests. Why? Because the Muslims are brethren in Islamic law, and even the lowest in rank among them may enter into a contract that is binding for all. They share each other's burdens and they advise each other.[1] Therefore, a person cannot do with his money that which may harm him in this world or the Hereafter. These limitations on financial freedom are

---

1 As it is narrated in a Hadith quoted by Abu Dawood (2751) on the authority of Amr bin Shu'aib, who narrated from his father and grandfather that the Messenger of Allah said: the Muslims are equal in their bloods, the lowest in rank among them may bear a responsibility that is binding for all and the most distant among them may give them protection. They are united against any outside force..."

rare. In most cases, people use their money as they wish for any legal purpose.

Another example of freedom is political freedom, which is generally understood in the West to refer to elections and democracy. Democratic elections can be conducted with justice or they can be swayed. Because who is the voter? The people. And you see now that in the developed countries that hold elections, the politicians use media campaigns to get ahead. Therefore, those who have money and can wage the strongest media campaign will win the election. They may not be the right people for the job, but the people elect them thinking that they are the right people.They deceive the people who do not know who to choose and who is good for them. People differ in their mental capabilities, some are not wise and do not know what is beneficial for the people and the nation as a whole, so some people can sway the elections results by paying huge amount of money. There are some Zionist lobbies that spend huge amount of money to affect the results of elections here and there so that they may bring in the person they want. In other words, the political freedom which is found in the form of holding elections and creating a parliament does not always serve the people's interests in their countries.

Regarding this issue in Islamic law, if we look at Islamic history and the application of Islam during the time of the rightly guided caliphs, it is seen that the issue of governance is left to the members of society known for their knowledge and experience. So in the issue of electing the governor and the caliph and choosing the best person for this job, Islamic law has not made the people equal. The most ignorant people are not made equal with the wisest people and the ones who do not know the rulings of Islamic law are not made equal with the scholars in choosing the governor by giving a right to vote to each one of them. Islamic law does not allow this. If equality is given in this sense, then it will lead to a catastrophe. Rather, Islamic law leaves this in the hands of the members of society known for their knowledge and experience. For this reason, Abu Bakr appointed Umar and Umar in turn appointed a consultative council from the members of society known for their knowledge and experience.

So the political freedoms which they claim and the parliaments and elections according to the present system are not held everywhere. Secondly, their interest at the first place is to please the people. Regarding their real interests, it is seen that many of the presidents and the key position holders in the western countries are not the best available but the people wanted them to be there.

In connection with the topic of political freedom according to their terminology, it appears that they mean by political freedom the right of every faction to form a political party that can grow among the people, become active, and then affect the general political scene according to the party's platform. Hence, we see many parties in western and eastern countries fighting with each other, like the Democratic Party, the Republican Party, the Socialist

Party, and the Labour Party.

These parties vie with each other, and when any one of them wins, it imposes its agenda, political ideology and judicial opinions on the entire population. So you see that the triumph of a particular party does not ensure political rights, neither does it ensure the consent of people. It only ensures the pleasure of the members of that party. The others remain unhappy, wishing that the winning party had never won. They condemn its actions and opinions.

Therefore,the application of political freedoms as they have them, creates competition between the political parties which does not lead the country to any government by consensus. It also does not make the people happy with the decisions taken by the state. Thus, a party can rule thanks to political and democratic freedoms but not be accepted by the people. You have many examples in front of you, like when some Islamic parties won in Algeria and Turkey, the state was not happy with it and opted for military rule instead. They wanted democracy and human rights, but when the Islamic parties won, it became unacceptable. Even the United Nations, the human rights organizations, and western countries do not practice the human rights they declare. If I start talking about the violations of the western countries and the United Nations regarding human rights in political freedoms, the list of violations would be very long.

Islamic law has come with something greater than what is mentioned above, something greater than every other experience in human history. This is the principle of sincere advice and advising the ones in authority with the intention of seeking Allah's pleasure. Advising those in authority is a legal obligation as our Prophet peace be upon him said: “Religion is but sincere advice.”

“We said: for whom O Messenger of Allah?”

He said: “For Allah, His Book, His Messenger, for the leaders of the Muslims and for the general public."[1]

Therefore, advising the Muslim leaders is an obligation. There is no good in them if they do not listen to the advice and there is no good in the believers if they do not advise them. The question is: how is this advice supposed to reach them? The channels of conveying the advice during early times of Islam were through the people of authority and consultative councils.

Regarding the freedom of religion, they say that people can choose any religion they want as long as they behave properly and commit no transgression against others. Regarding the religion of Allah which He has revealed upon His Messenger - Islam - it is the true religion. If people choose Islam as their religion and then decide to say: "I am free to choose any other religion", it is not allowed for them. Why? Because they have become like

1- Narrated by Imam Muslim (55) and by Imam Bukhari in the Book of Iman, Chapter on the saying of the Prophet peace be upon him: Religion is but sincere advice, for Allah, His Book, His Messenger, for the leaders of the Muslims and for the general public.

insane people who do not know what is good for them. Their betterment is in the religion of Islam in this world and in the Hereafter. If we allow them to leave the religion, we allow them to be among the people of Fire. This is why whoever leaves Islam is killed as it is narrated from the Prophet in an authentic hadith: "Whoever changes his religion, kill him."[1]

So if a Muslim in an Islamic state chooses any religion other than Islam, the death penalty is legally incumbent upon the state:

﴿... مَن يَرْتَدَّ مِنكُمْ عَن دِينِهِۦ فَسَوْفَ يَأْتِي ٱللَّهُ بِقَوْمٍ يُحِبُّهُمْ وَيُحِبُّونَهُۥٓ ...﴾ [المائدة: ٥٤]

"Whoever from among you turns back from his religion (Islam), Allah will bring a people whom He will love and they will love Him."[2]

1- Narrated by Imam Bukhari (6922).

[2] *al-Mā'idah: 54*

Regarding the non-Muslims, they may choose any religion they like. We do not force people to become believers. The Prophet allowed the Jews and Christians to remain on their religions, but he continued inviting them to Islam. He had the authority to order them or prohibit them, but he never forced them. They were given the option to remain on their religion.

So religious freedom is guaranteed, provided the conversion is not from Islam to any other religion, because Islam is the true religion and Islamic law has come to protect the interests of the people. Converting from this religion shows that the person who does so is unwise.

Among the freedoms that are mentioned, which Islam does not grant in and unlimited form, is the freedom of expression. Generally, it means that all people are free to publicly express any opinion they have or say whatever they think without any accountability.

In Islamic law, this is not correct. Islamic law does not allow anyone to say anything they want to say. People differ in their mental capabilities, while Islamic law has come to bring the people into the grace of Allah, and the people are also not equal in their understanding, so if they are allowed to spread any doubtful thing, then it is very much possible that a person of weak faith who is uneducated and unable to rebut that doubtful thing from Satan, will be misguided. When it is made public, it will surely lead to many great evils.

During the reign of Umar, a man from the tribe of Banu Ghunaim named Sabeegh bin Isl, came to Madina. He had some books with him and started asking people about the parables in the Qur'an. The news reached Umar, so he called him and prepared some sticks from the branches of a date tree for him. When he entered and sat, Umar asked him who he was. He said: "I am the servant of Allah Sabeegh." Umar said: "And I am the servant of Allah Umar" and then started beating that man with the stick until his head started bleeding.

The man said: “Enough O Commander of the Faithful, I swear upon Allah that the doubts I had in my head have gone."[1]

This man Sabeegh was roaming among the people with questions regarding the parables in Qur'an, asking what is meant by statements like: “By those [winds] scattering [dust] dispersing” and “Those [clouds] carrying a load [of water].” Umar punished him for asking this kind of question and spreading doubts among the people. Umar also sent him into exile and ordered that he should not mingle with the people so that they would not be affected by his misguidance. The great aim Umar had in front of him was the aim for which the Messengers were sent: to bring the people into the grace of their Lord.

So if there is someone who wants to spread whatever comes to their mind and spoil the religion

---

1This story was narrated by al-Aajuri in al-Sharia (p 153), Ibn Batta in al-Ibana (p 789) and al-Lalakai in Sharh Usool I'tiqad Ahl al-Sunnah wa al-Jama'ah (4/706).

of the people, it is considered against the principle for which the Messengers were sent. Our Prophet was sent with Islam to bring the people into the grace of their Lord and to establish the truth of Islam through devotion to Allah, the Lord of the universe.

So if a person tries to breach this principle or dig underneath the foundations to demolish the edifice of faith, even by spreading doubtful things, it becomes incumbent to stop him. Hence, Islam does not give unlimited freedom in expressing one's opinion. You may give your opinions as long as they do not defame the Holy Qur'an, the Sunnah, and Islamic principles.

If a person comes with ideas that defame the religion, detract from its sanctity, or encourage people to distance themselves from the worship of Allah, that person's actions are repugnant to the purpose of sending the Prophet, which is to bring people into the grace of Allah.

We are unequal in our capabilities. The majority of the people are emotional. They are not people of distinction who understand matters through logic, evidence, and the judicious analysis of benefits and harms. The majority of the people are emotional, swayed this way and that by persuasive speaking. Sometimes, even a judge, in cases where there is insufficient evidence, may make a mistake if one of the litigants is more eloquent than the other in presenting his case, and give a verdict based on what he hears.

The Prophet said: "You come to me with your cases, and it is very much possible that one of you is more eloquent than the other in presenting his case, so if I give a verdict based on what he says and give him what is actually the right of his brother, then I am giving him a piece of fire, and he should not take it."[1]

Opening wide the door of freedom of opinion may affect the peoples' religion, spoiling their religious commitment, weakening their Islam, and removing the effects of the Messenger's mission to

1 Narrated by Imam Bukhari (2680) and Imam Muslim (1713).

humanity by turning the people away from being content with the religion of Allah.

You may see now in the countries where this door of various opinions is opened, how the people are affected with these thoughts and how many of them have turned their back on religion. May Allah save us and protect us.

Many people, as I have said, are emotional and accept what is said to them without any clarification. They do not know the other viewpoint. It is the duty of the scholars to explain to the people the vain talk of every corrupt person in order to protect their religion and to rebut the doubts that are spread, but this not always possible. So if complete freedom of opinion is granted, it will lead to the corruption of people's beliefs and since they are not capable of repelling the doubts that are instigated.

Hence we may say that Islamic law has come to protect human rights regardless whether this human is a father or child, husband or wife, caliph or subject, judge or judged, governor or governed, ruler or subject, boss or servant, male or female.

It should be clear from what preceded that Islamic law has come to protect all these rights. It should also be clear that it has guaranteed the rights of all people, like the rights of parents, children, spouses, Muslims, and non-Muslims. The non-Muslim neighbour has rights upon the Muslim neighbour. The one who is under protection also has rights. It is narrated from Abdullah bin Umar that he slaughtered a sheep then asked: "Have you sent meat as a gift to my Jewish neighbour? I have heard the Messenger of Allah saying: 'The angel Gabriel kept on advising me on the rights of the neighbour so much that I thought that he would give him rights to inherit."[1] This is due to the general benefit secured for the community through honouring the rights of the neighbour.

Islamic law has guaranteed all rights, financial and civil, just as it has guaranteed freedoms, but

---

1 Narrated by Abu Dawood (5152), Tirmidhi (1943), Ahmad (11/38), Bukhari (6014, 6015) and Muslim (2624, 2625).

within the limits that serve the considerations of human welfare that it seeks to uphold.

It should be kept in mind that Islamic law did not come to serve worldly interests only; rather it came to serve the interests of this world and the Hereafter. So it secures the good of this life and of the life after death.

In these brief pages, I have mentioned the crux of the important topic of human rights. What I have mentioned cannot address all aspects of the topic, but it opens the door to understanding this term which is repeated so frequently. It should be believed that any country where Islamic law is revered and applied, that country will be the most protective of human rights. If the application of Islamic law becomes weak in any country, it will be weak in realising human rights. For this reason, human rights are connected with the application of Islamic law in people's lives. If the judicial rights, financial rights, justice between the people, and lawful freedoms are enjoyed by the people, it means that the people have taken their rights as a society and as individuals.

It is well known that the perfect realisation of human rights was during the time of Prophet Muhammad and during the time of rightly guided Caliphs who came after him. Then in each and every country of Islam, be it the era of the Umayyads or Abbasids, whenever the application of Islamic law was stronger, the protection of human rights was greater.

These have been a few brief statements concerning a vast topic.

I ask Allah to make us among those who invite to His religion, who show patience and perseverance and make us among those who help His law. Make us among those who seek knowledge and convey it. Make us among those who defend the Sunnah of the leader of the Messengers and who defend the law of the Lord of the universe. Certainly Allah is the most generous and most noble.

I ask Allah to forgive me my sins and your sins. O Allah! Forgive us our sins and shortcomings. Be with us and do not be against us. O Allah! Provide us with guidance in all matters. Make faith as beloved to us, and beautify it in our hearts, and make disbelief, sin and disobedience hateful to us and make us among the guided ones. O Allah! We ask you to make us among those who follow the truth and uphold the faith. O Allah! Give us the ability to do that which pleases you and avoid that which makes you angry. You are the most generous among those who are generous. O Allah! Give the Muslim scholars the ability to rebut the plots of the plotters and to support the religion. Guide them in their words and deeds and reward them with a good reward. Grant our rulers the ability to do that which pleases You and make us and them to help each other in righteousness and piety. Provide them with pious companions who will lead them to righteousness and encourage them towards it. Keep them away from bad companions who advise them to do evil and encourage them to do it. Certainly You are the noblest among those who are noble and the most generous among the generous.

May Allah send His peace and blessings upon the trustworthy Prophet and upon his family and companions.

CPSIA information can be obtained
at www.ICGtesting.com
Printed in the USA
LVHW081159140722
723448LV00015B/214

9 787078 204073